He started to look
for some food.

Sie machte sich auf den Weg,
um Futter zu suchen.

One Sunday morning the warm sun came up and – pop! – out of the egg
came a tiny and very hungry caterpillar.

Und als an einem schönen Sonntagmorgen die Sonne aufging, hell und warm,
da schlüpfte aus dem Ei – knack – eine kleine hungrige Raupe.

In the light of the moon
a little egg lay on a leaf.

Nachts,
im Mondschein,
lag auf einem Blatt
ein kleines Ei.

For my sister Christa

Für meine Schwester Christa

On Monday he ate
through one apple.
But he was still
hungry.

Am Montag fraß
sie sich durch
einen Apfel, aber
satt war sie noch
immer nicht.

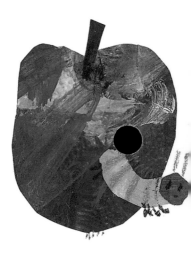

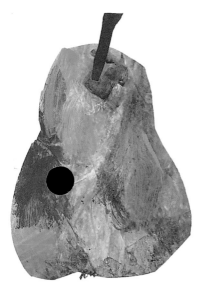

On Tuesday he ate
through two pears,
but he was still
hungry.

Am Dienstag fraß
sie sich durch zwei
Birnen, aber satt
war sie noch immer
nicht.

On Wednesday he
ate through three
plums, but he was
still hungry.

Am Mittwoch fraß
sie sich durch drei
Pflaumen, aber
satt war sie noch
immer nicht.

On Thursday he
ate through four
strawberries, but he
was still hungry.

Am Donnerstag
fraß sie sich durch
vier Erdbeeren,
aber satt war sie
noch immer nicht.

On Friday he ate
through five oranges,
but he was still
hungry.

Am Freitag fraß
sie sich durch fünf
Apfelsinen, aber
satt war sie noch
immer nicht.

On Saturday he ate through
one piece of chocolate cake, one ice-cream cone, one pickle, one slice of Swiss cheese, one slice of salami,

Am Sonnabend fraß sie sich durch
ein Stück Schokoladenkuchen, eine Eiswaffel, eine saure Gurke, eine Scheibe Käse, ein Stück Wurst,

one lollipop, one piece of cherry pie, one sausage, one cupcake, and one slice of watermelon.

einen Lolli, ein Stück Früchtebrot, ein Würstchen, ein Törtchen und ein Stück Melone.

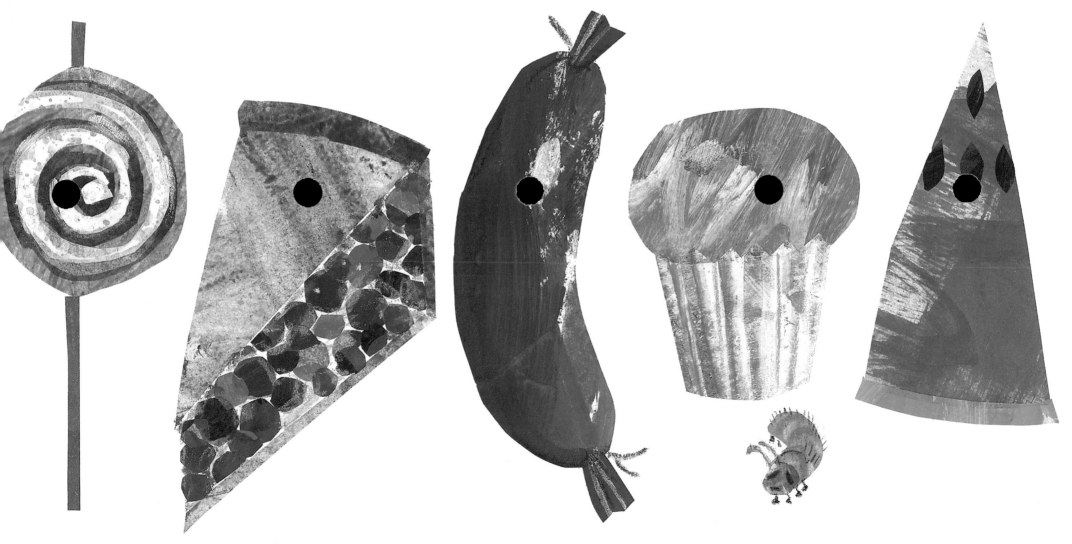

That night he had a stomachache!   An diesem Abend hatte sie Bauchschmerzen!

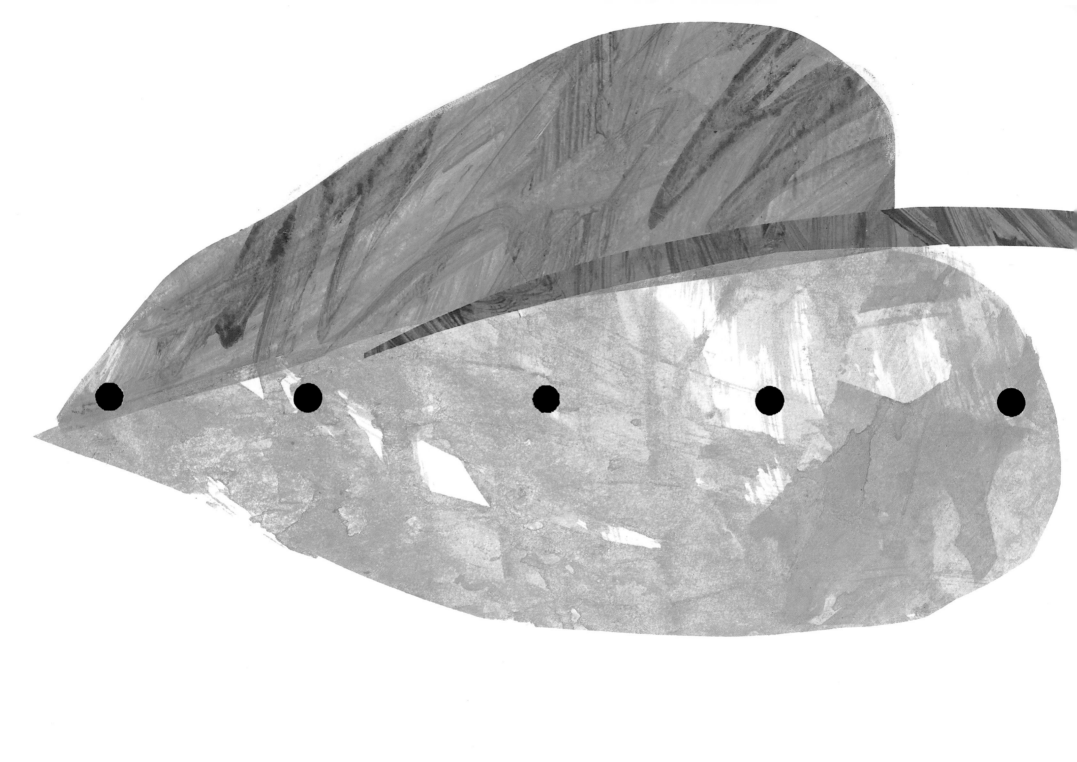

The next day was Sunday again.
The caterpillar ate through one nice green leaf,
and after that he felt much better.

Der nächste Tag war wieder ein Sonntag.
Die Raupe fraß sich durch ein grünes Blatt.
Es ging ihr nun viel besser.

Now he wasn't hungry any more – and he wasn't a little caterpillar any more. He was a big, fat caterpillar.

Sie war nicht mehr hungrig, sie war richtig satt.
Und sie war auch nicht mehr klein,
sie war groß und dick geworden.

He built a small house, called a cocoon, around himself. He stayed inside for more than two weeks.
Then he nibbled a hole in the cocoon, pushed his way out and ...

Sie baute sich ein enges Haus, das man Kokon nennt, und blieb darin
mehr als zwei Wochen lang. Dann knabberte
sie sich ein Loch in den Kokon, zwängte
sich nach draußen und ...

he was a beautiful butterfly!

war ein wunderschöner
Schmetterling!

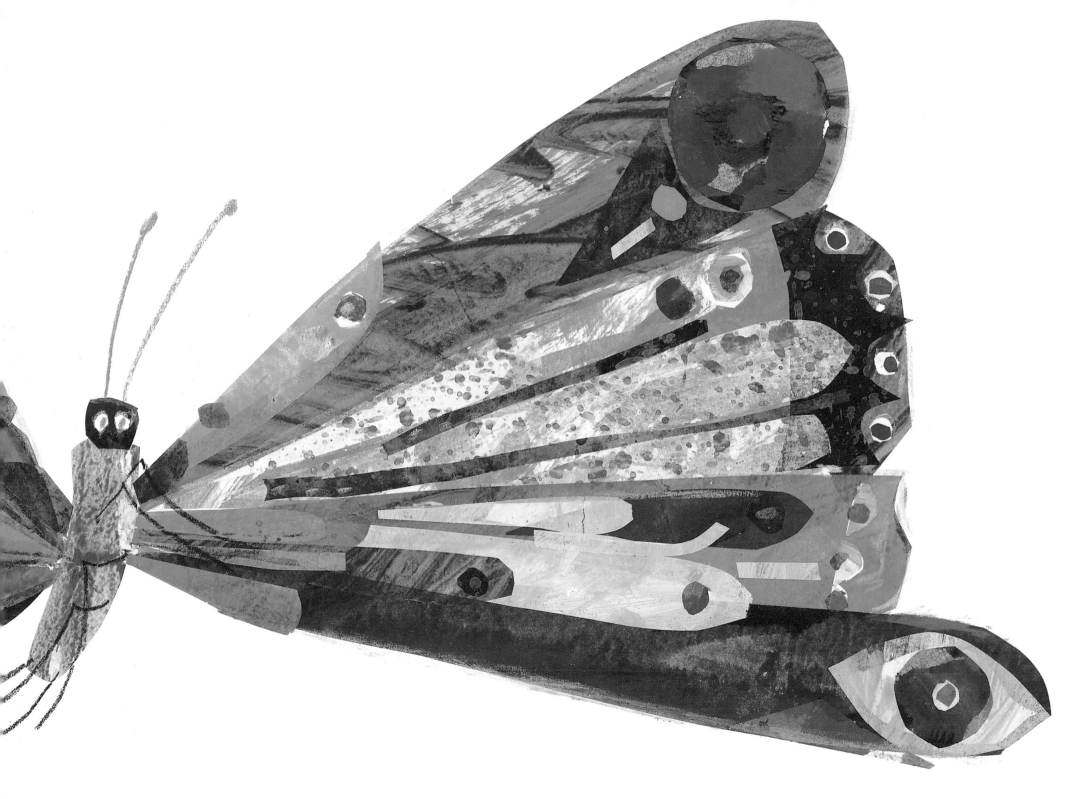

Eric Carle was born in 1929 in Syracuse, New York. From 1935 to 1952 he lived in Germany and then returned to the United States. In 1968 he published his first picture book and a year later his international career as an author and illustrator of children's books began. He is living in Florida and North Carolina. Eric Carle's books are published in German by Gerstenberg.

Eric Carle wurde 1929 in Syracuse, New York, geboren. Von 1935 bis 1952 lebte er in Deutschland und kehrte dann in die USA zurück. 1968 veröffentlichte er sein erstes Bilderbuch und begründete im Jahr darauf mit der „Kleinen Raupe Nimmersatt" seine internationale Karriere als Kinderbuchautor und -illustrator. Er lebt in Florida und North Carolina.
Eric Carles Bücher erscheinen auf Deutsch bei Gerstenberg.

Mehr über Eric Carle, die kleine Raupe Nimmersatt & Co finden Sie in der Rubrik *Kindergarten und Schule* unter **www.gerstenberg-verlag.de** und **www.eric-carle.com**

10. Auflage 2017
Copyright © 1969 Eric Carle
Zweisprachige Ausgabe
Copyright © 2004 Gerstenberg Verlag, Hildesheim
Aus dem Englischen übertragen von Viktor Christen
Alle Rechte vorbehalten
Druck und Bindung: TBB, a. s., Banská Bystrica
Printed in the Slovak Republic
ISBN 978-3-8369-5055-8

Eric Carle

The Very Hungry Caterpillar

Die kleine Raupe Nimmersatt

GERSTENBERG